Mazes

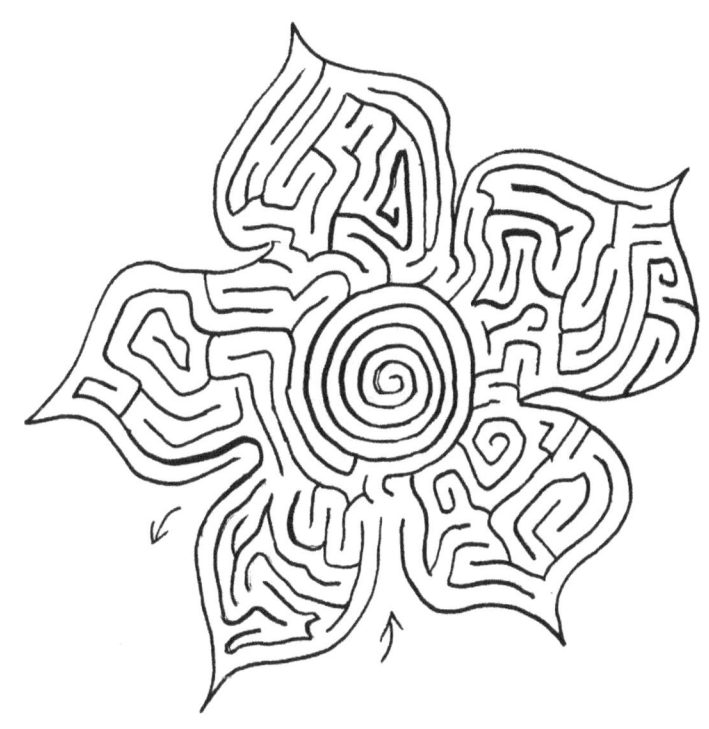

FLOWER

D.E.W. 2006

Daisy Eliza Wrightson

All-square

10-15 min

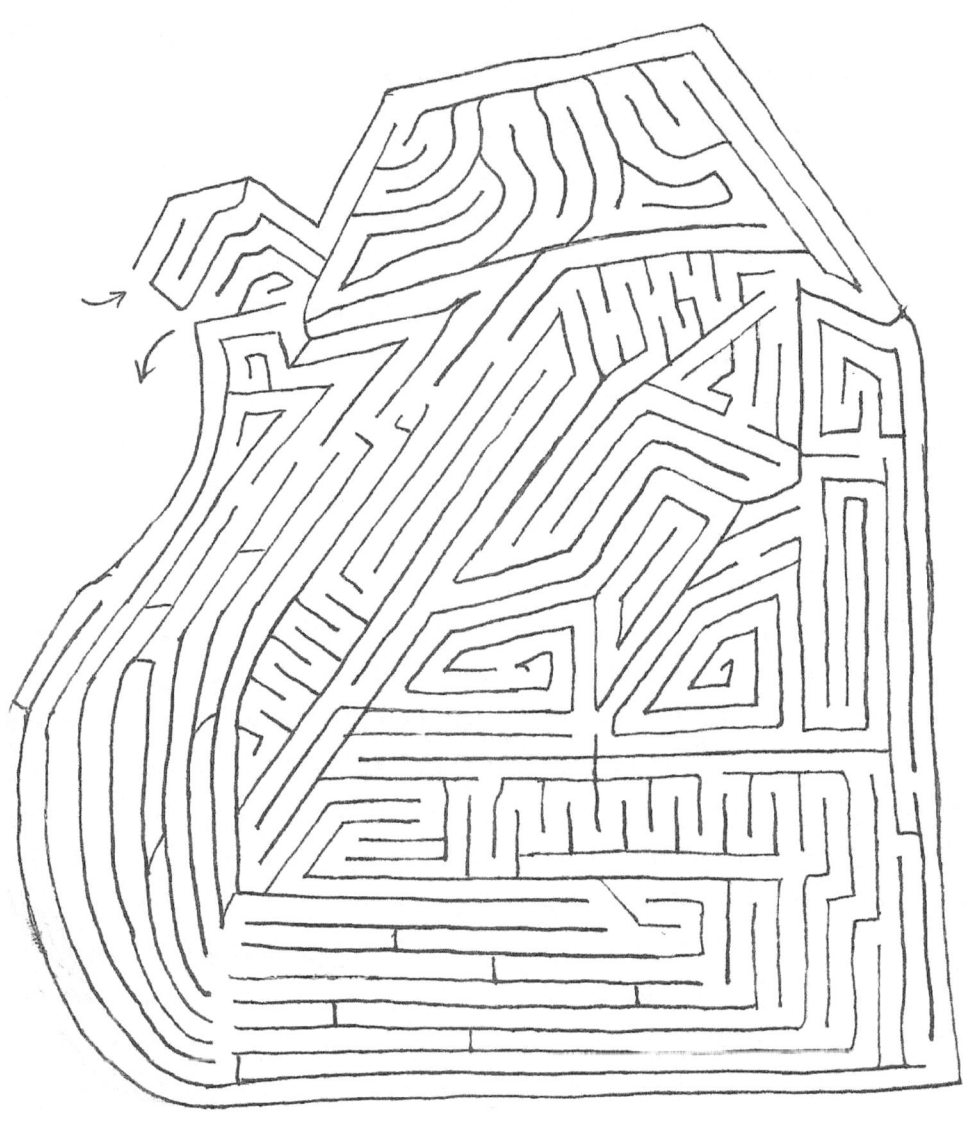

All −square

D.E. Wrightson 2011

Coffee table

8-10 min

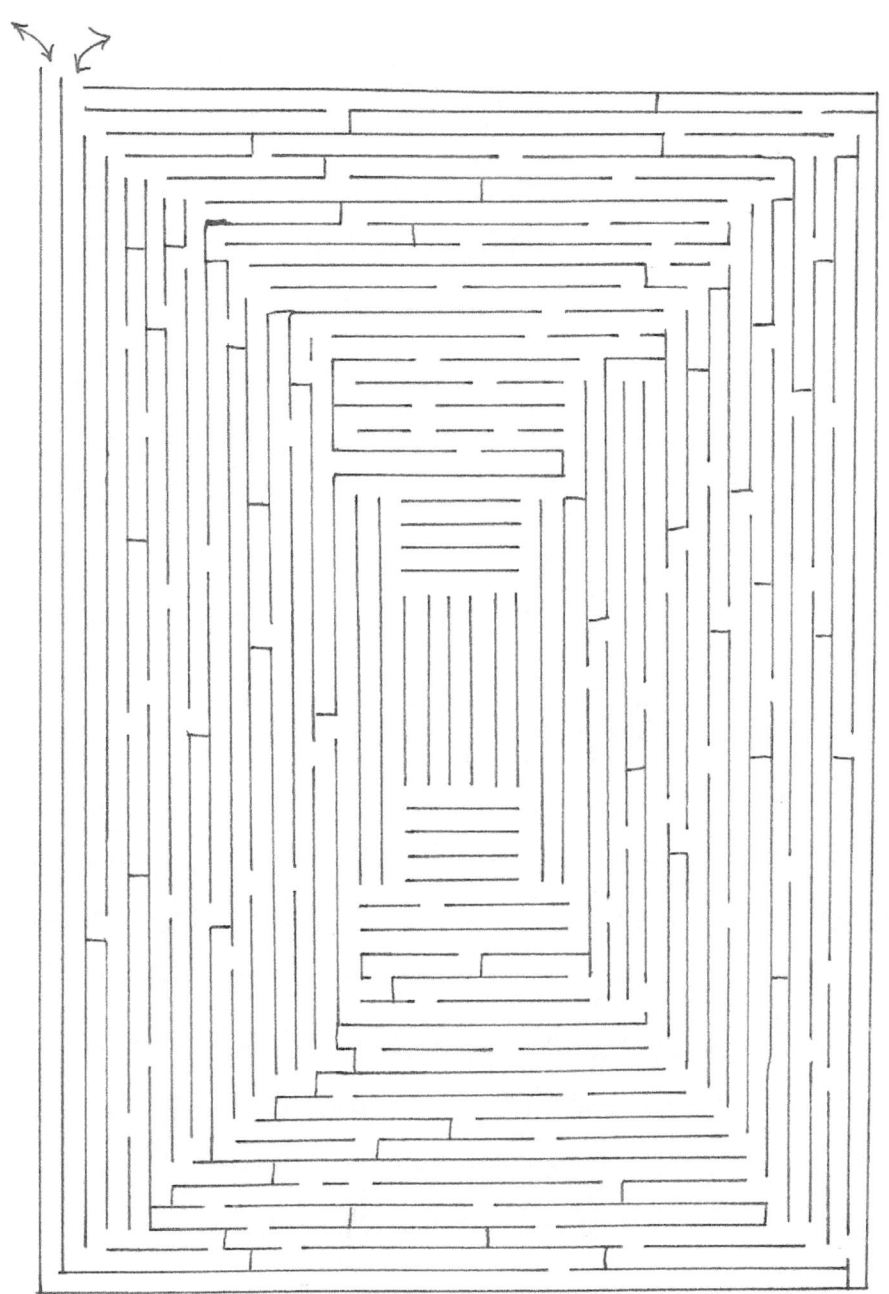

D.E.W. 2013

Coffee table

Cat on a cushion

10-15 min

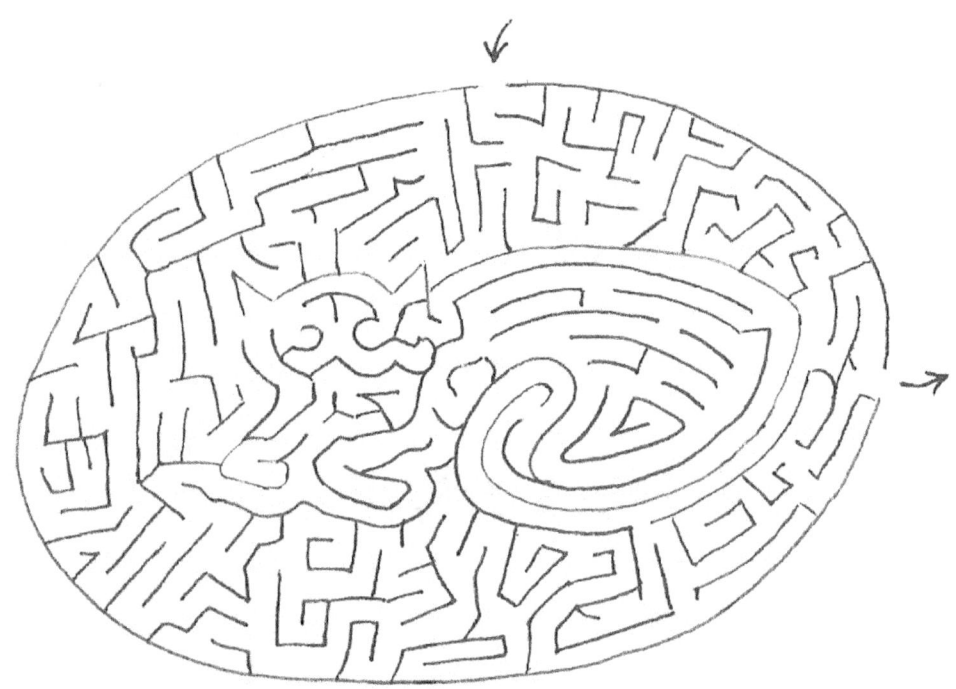

Cat on a cushion

DW

Brain

10-15 min

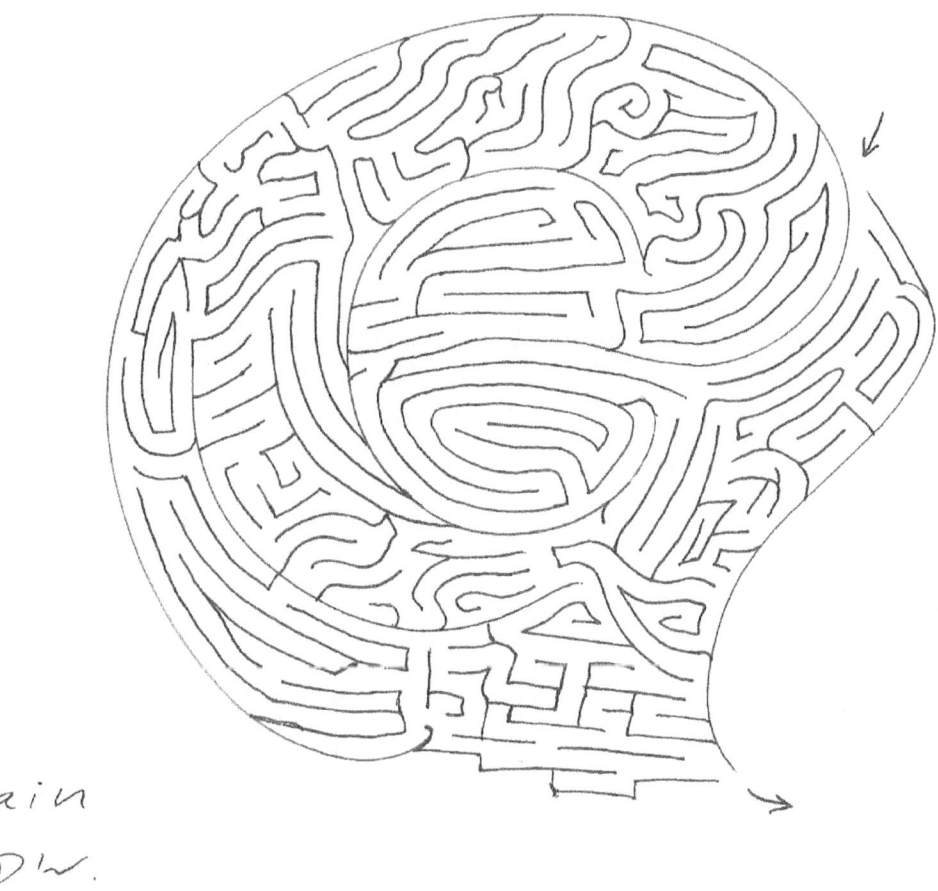

Brain
DW.

Anger

10-15 min

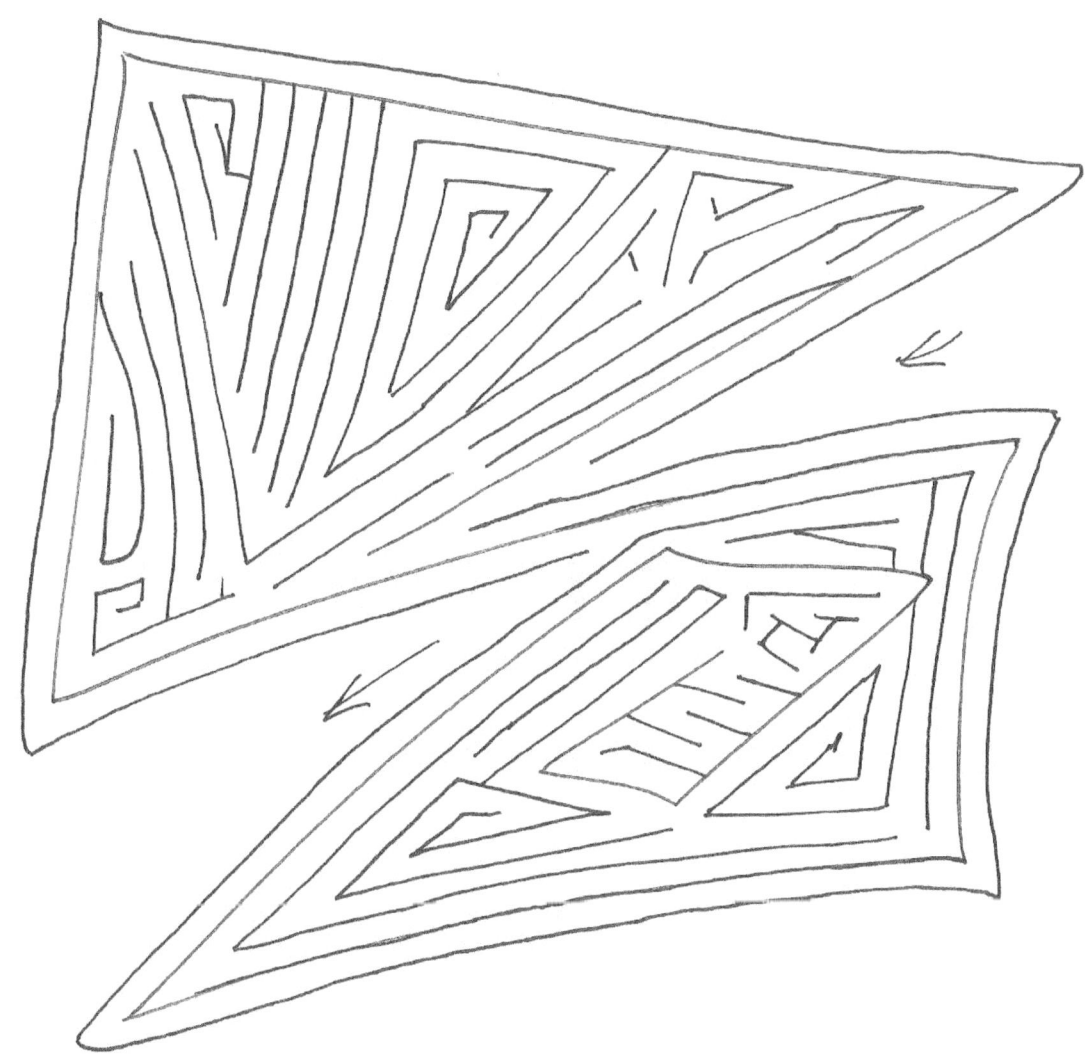

Anger

D. W.

Dolf .. - what?

10-15 min

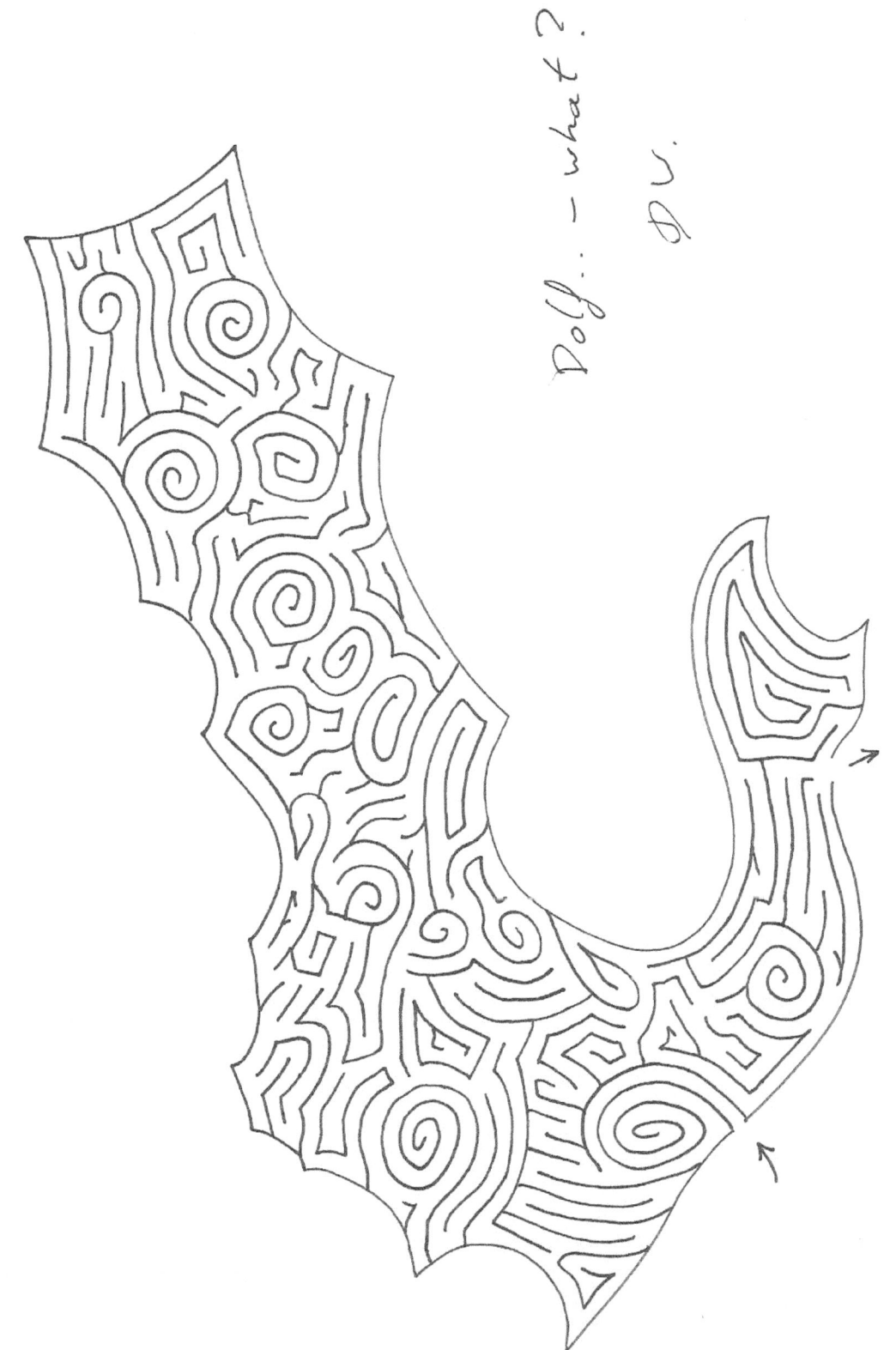

Dolf... — what?
Du.

Water Drop on a Leaf

10-15 min

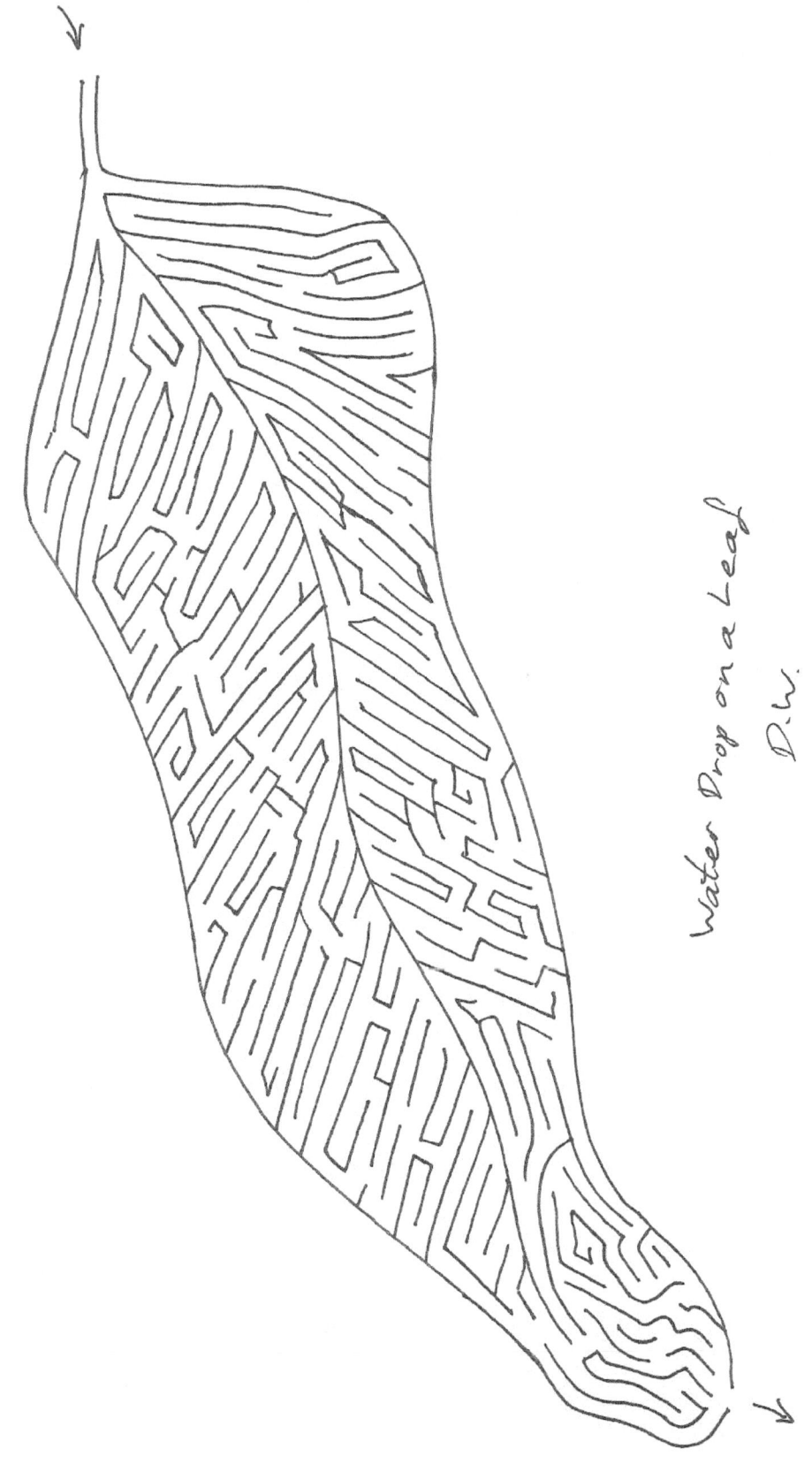

Water Drop on a Leaf

D.W.

Dog-Leg

10-15 min

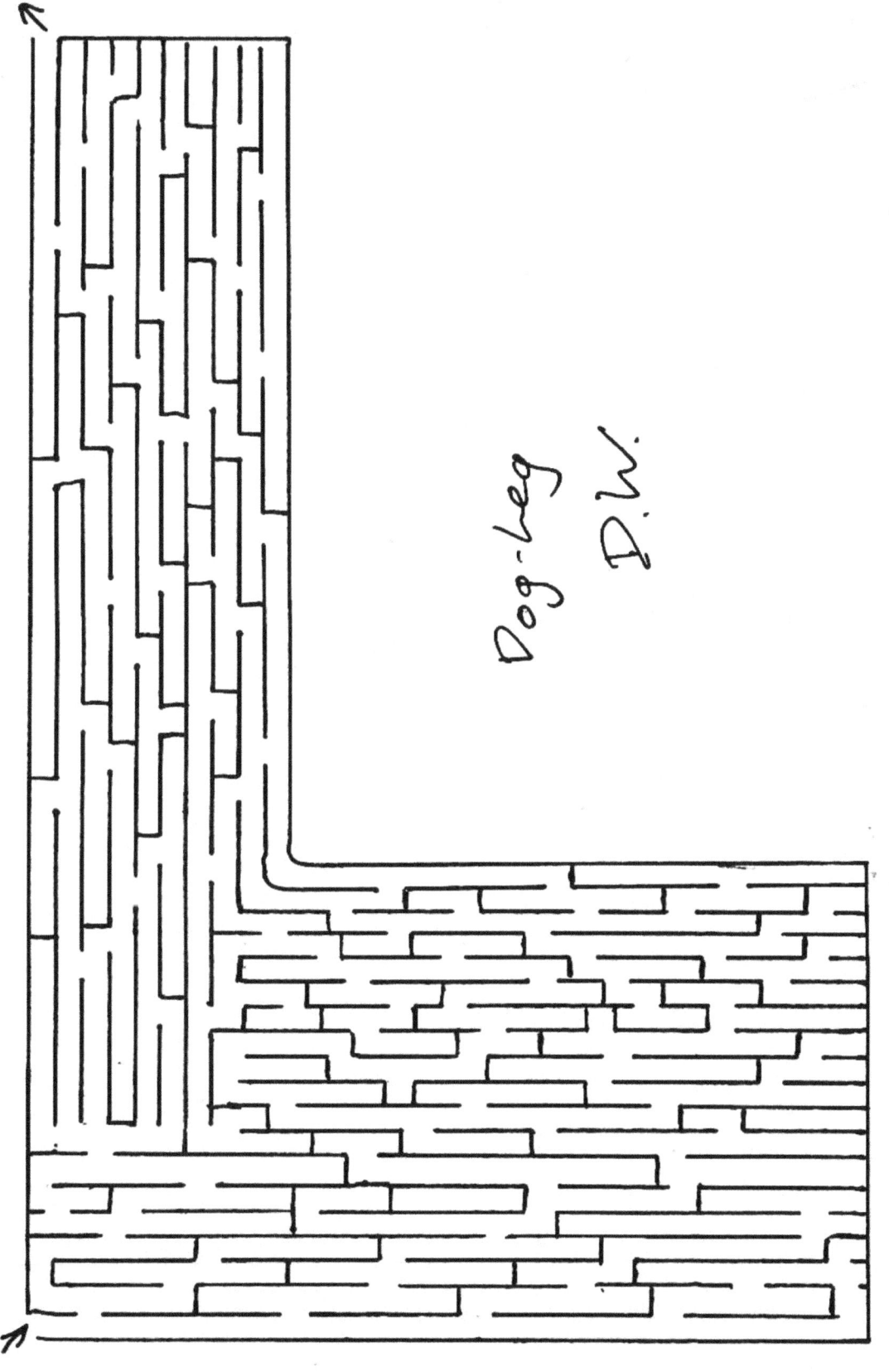

Dog-leg
D.W.

Flutterbye

10-15 min

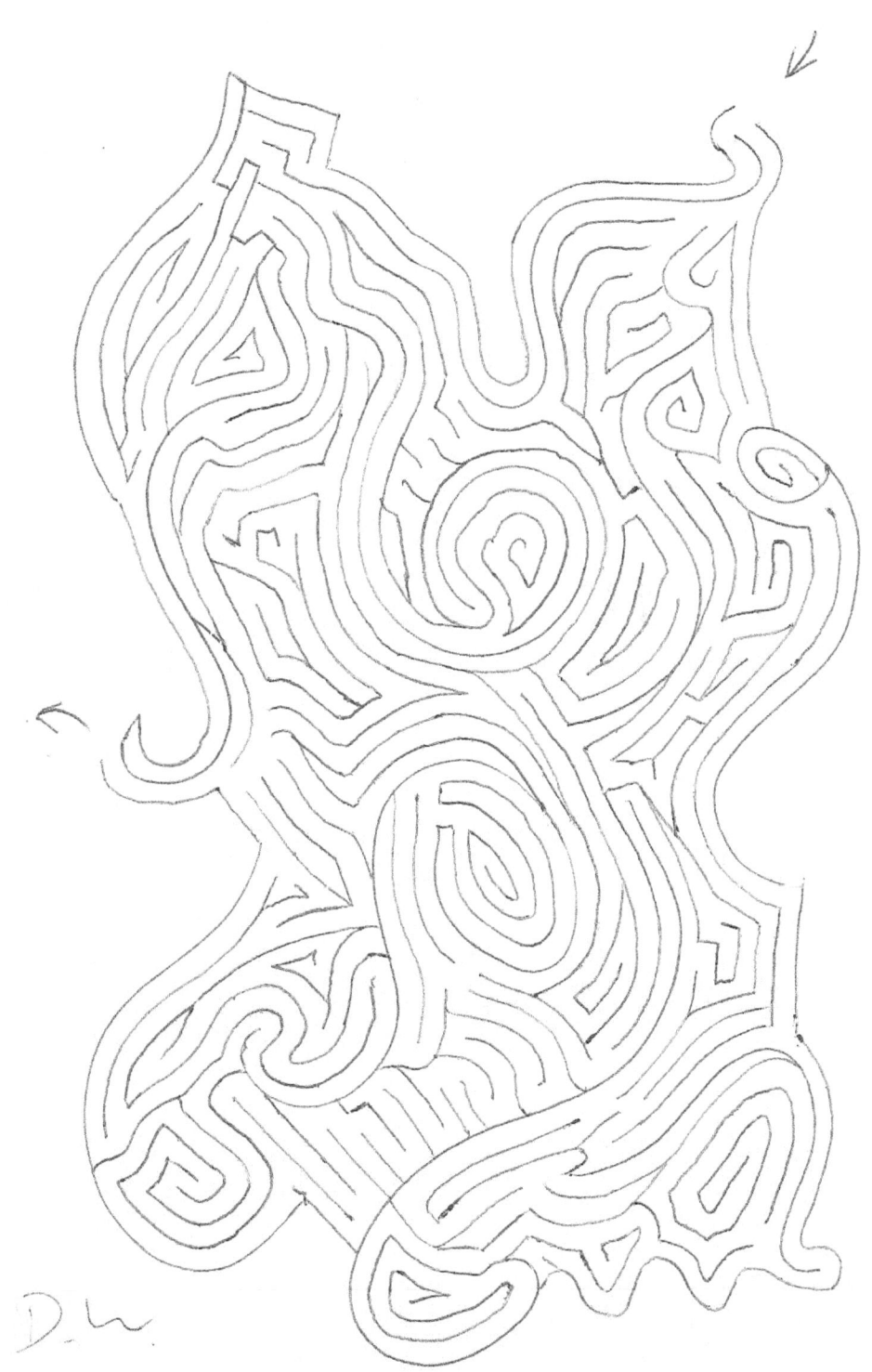

D.W.

Jimmied

10-15 min

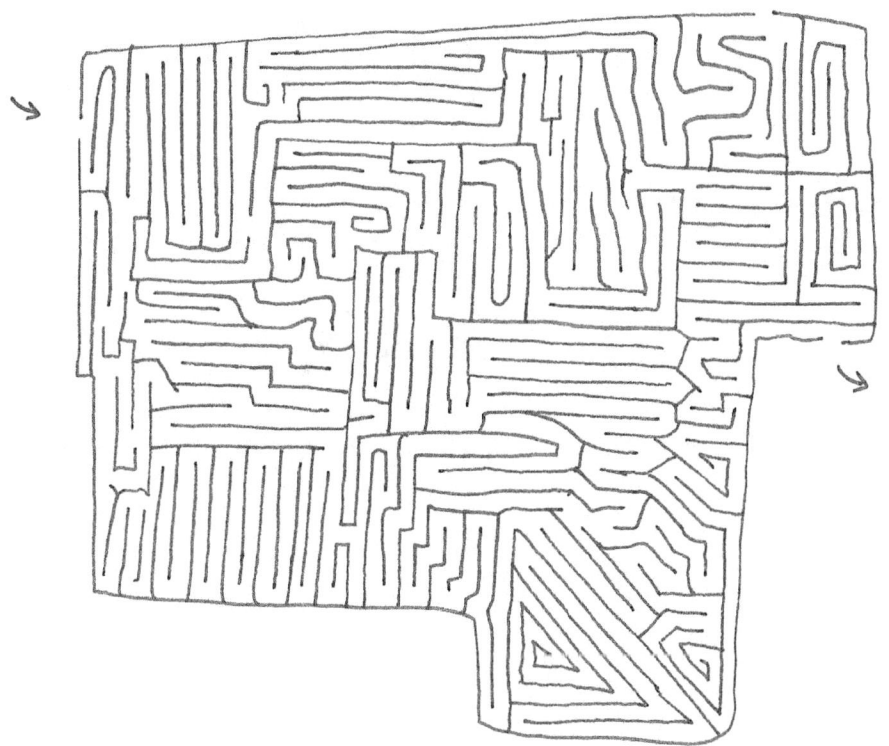

D. S.W.
2006

Eggy

10-15 min

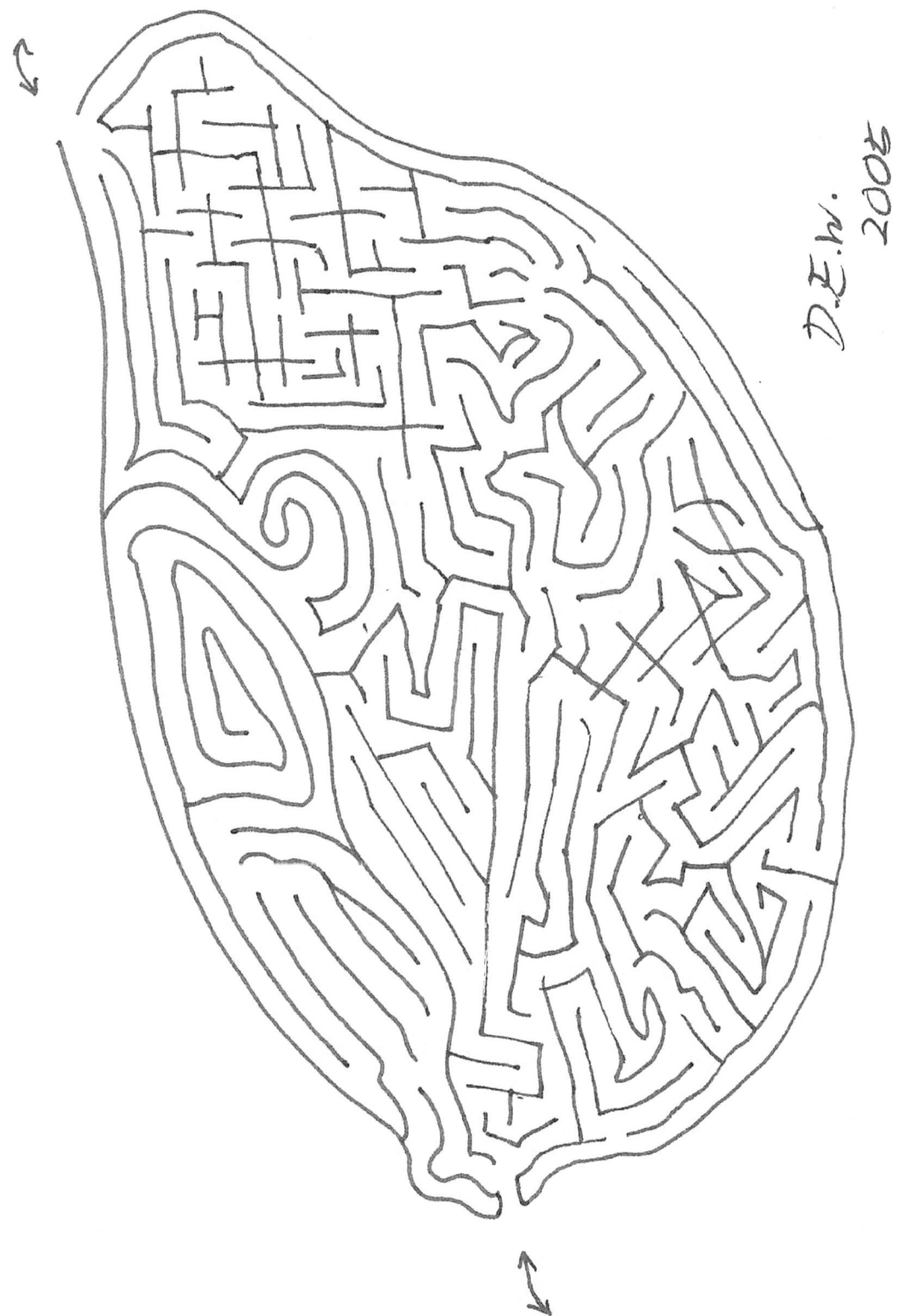

D.E.W.
2005

Fritillarys

20-25 min

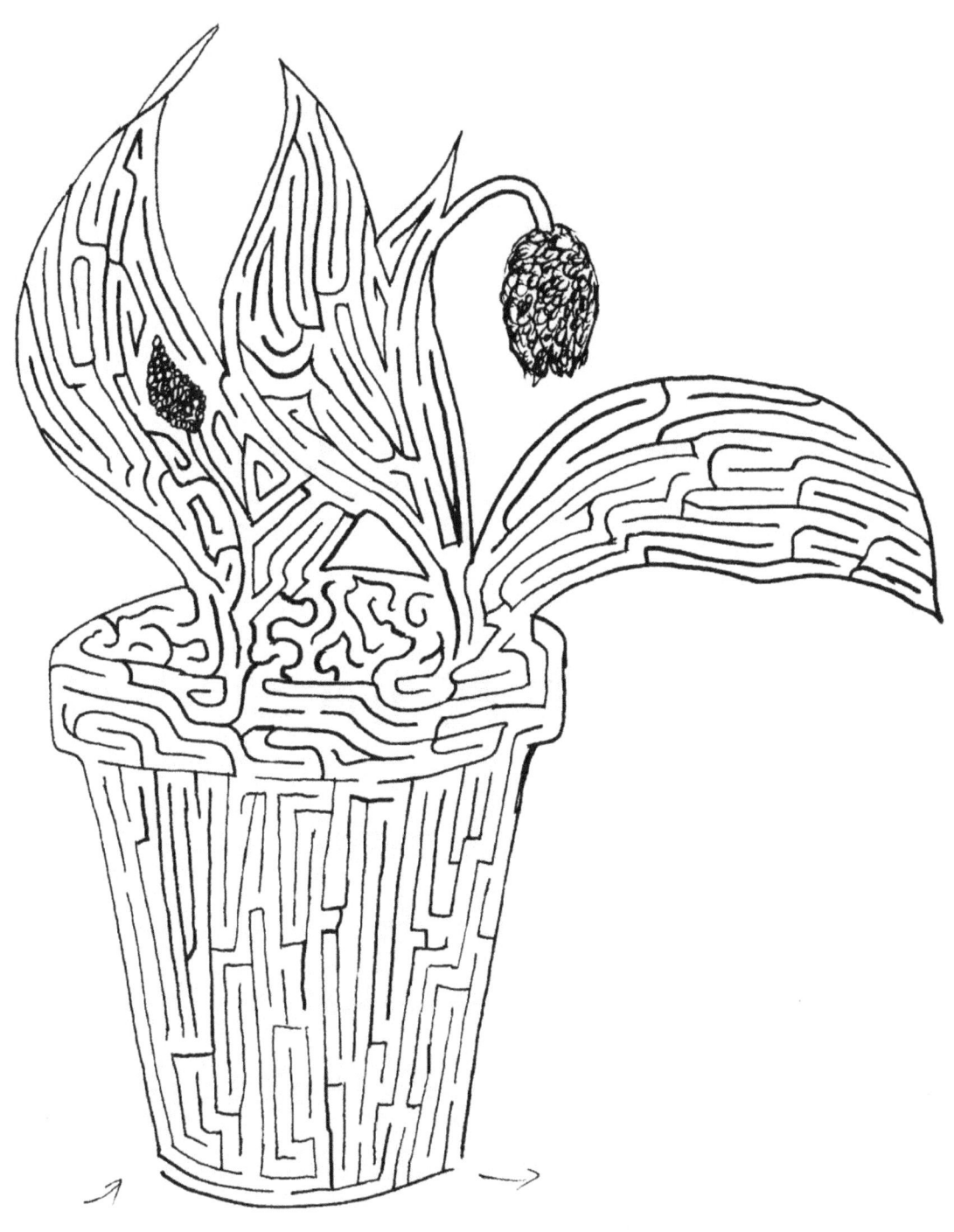

Fritillarys

DEW 2006

Handkerchief

20-25 min

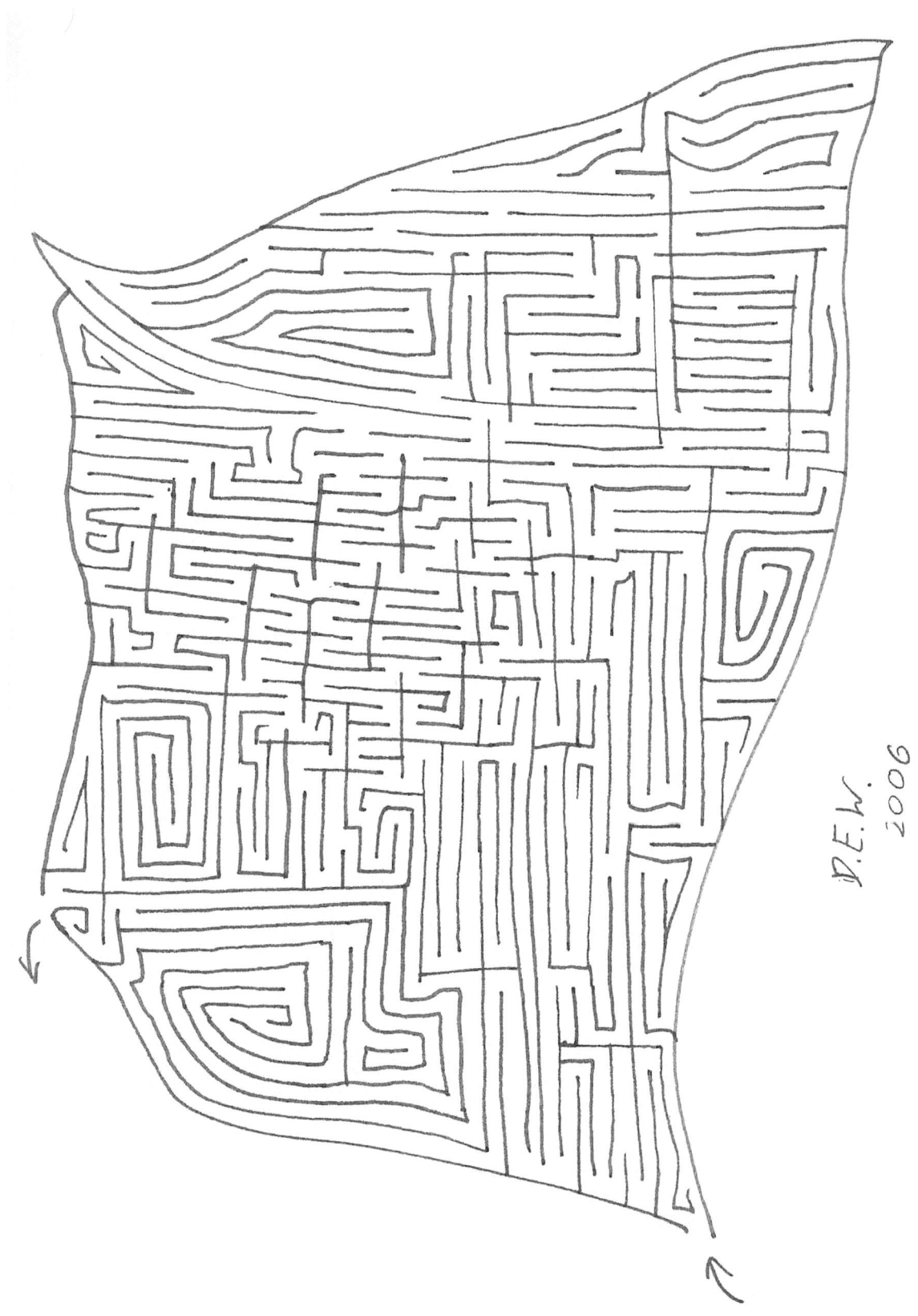

D.E.W.
2006

Cockerel

25-30 min

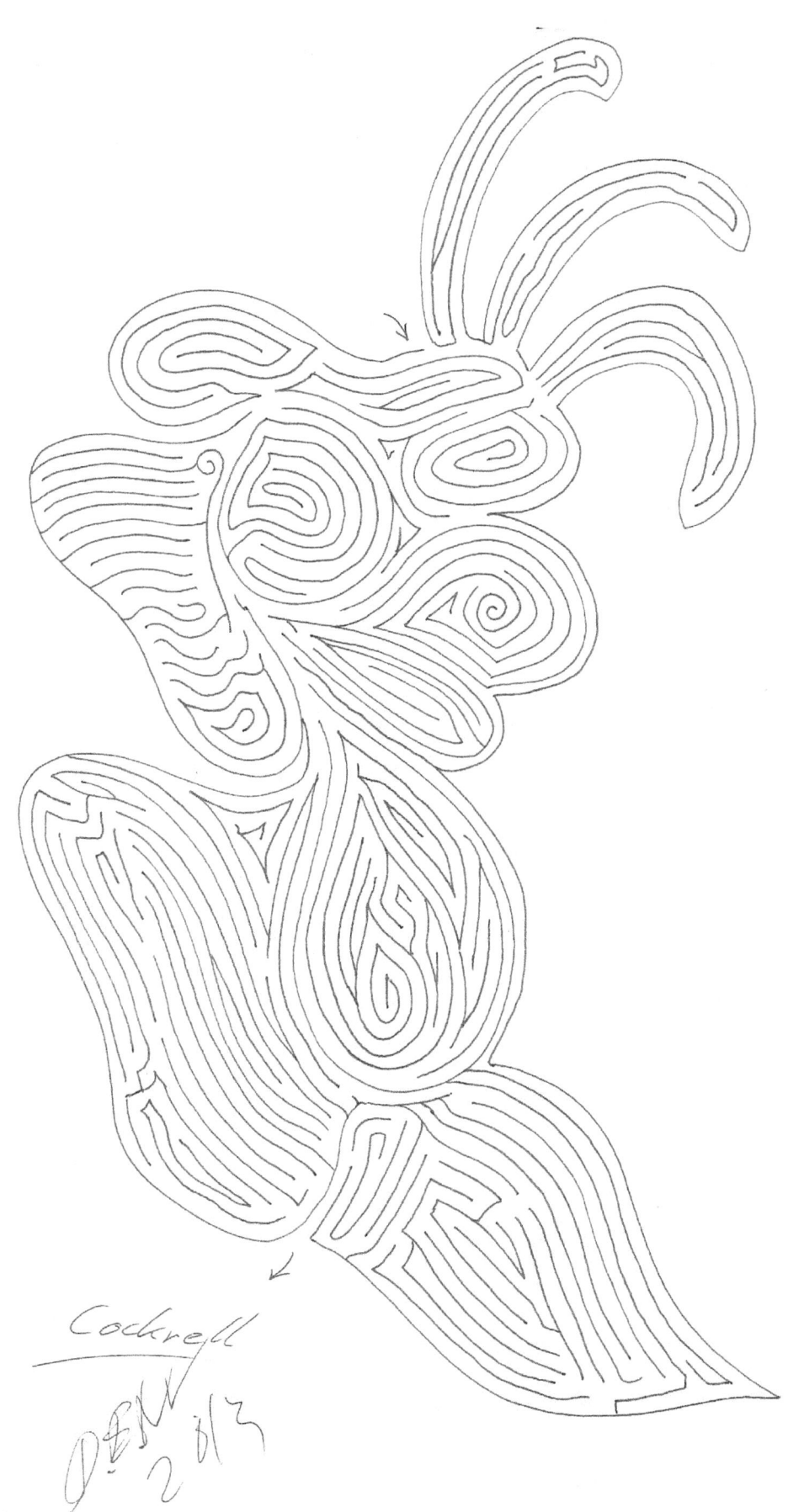

Cockrell
DEW 2013

Head

25-30 min

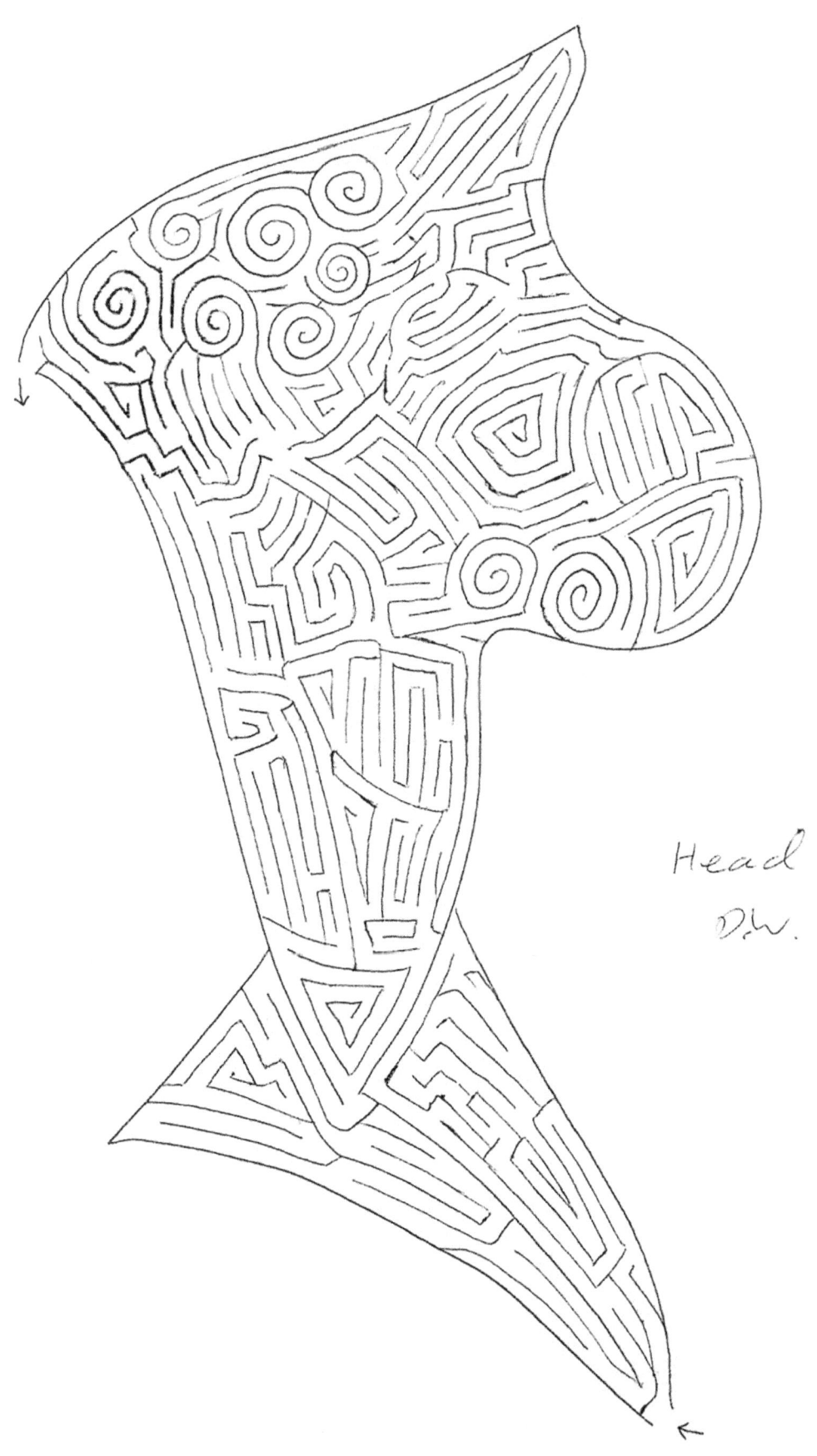

Head
D.W.

Bindweed

30-35 min

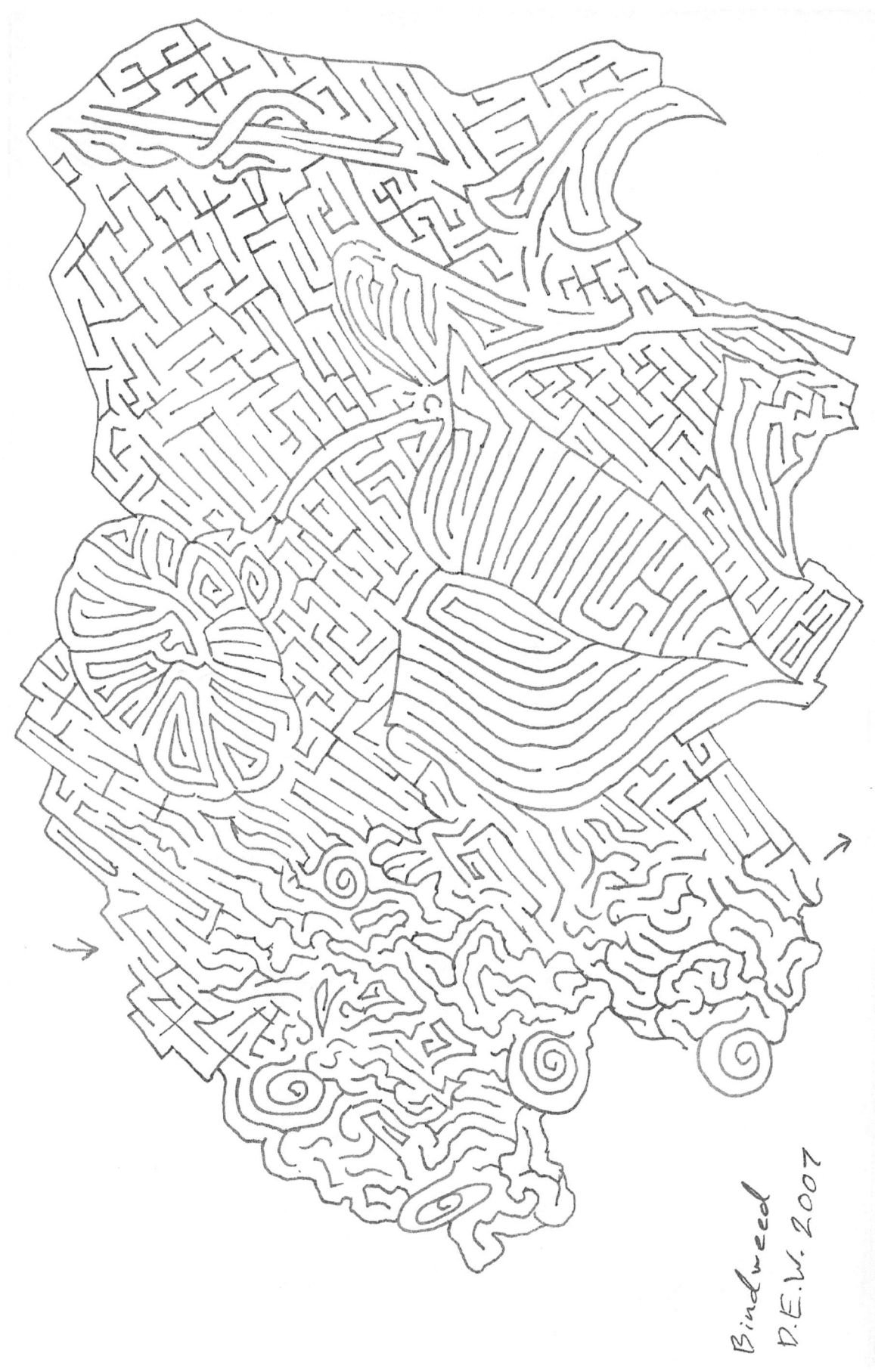

Bindweed
D.E.W. 2007

Bug Face

30-35 min

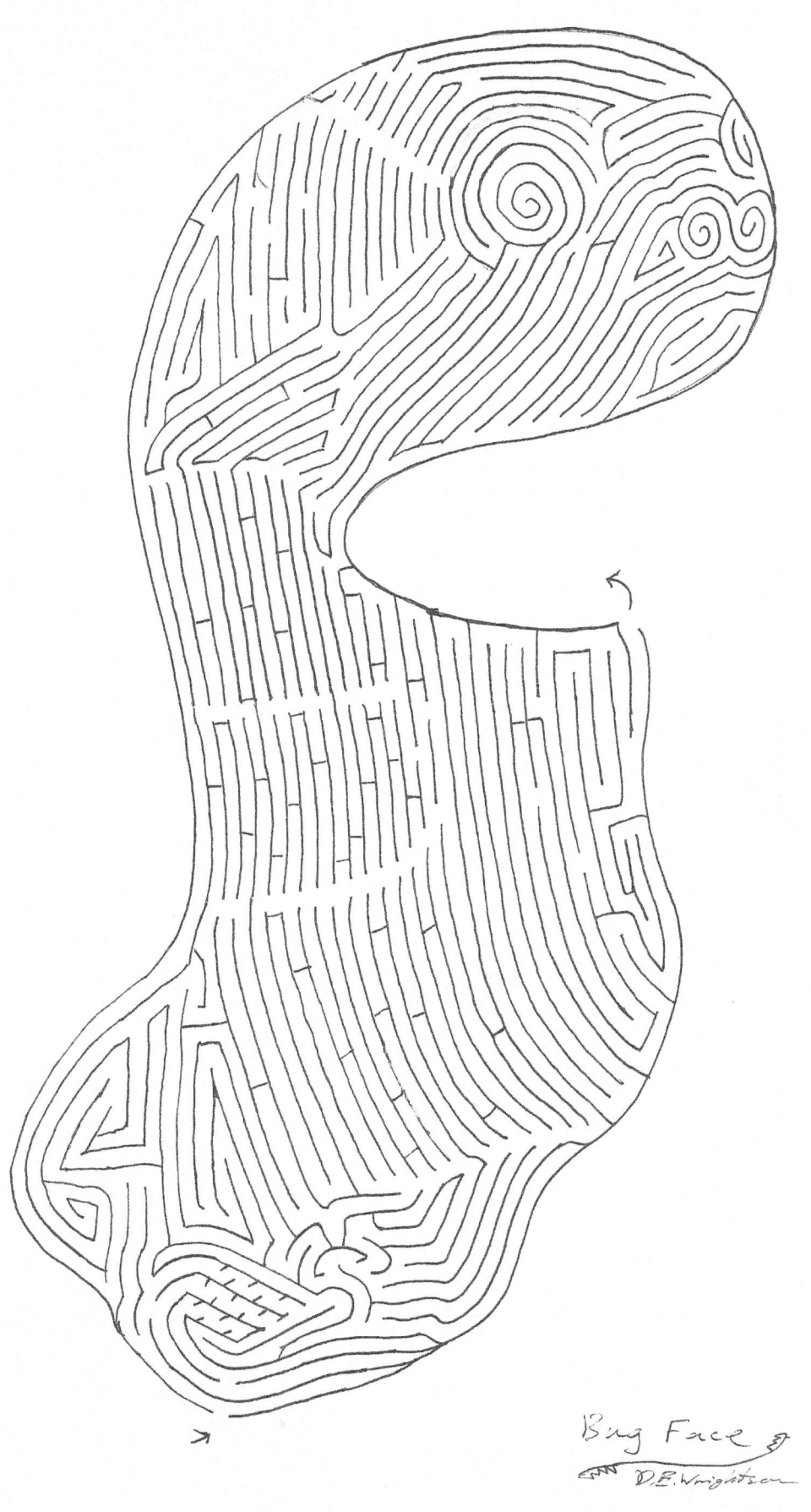

Bug Face
D.E. Wrightson

Ink Swirly

15-20 min

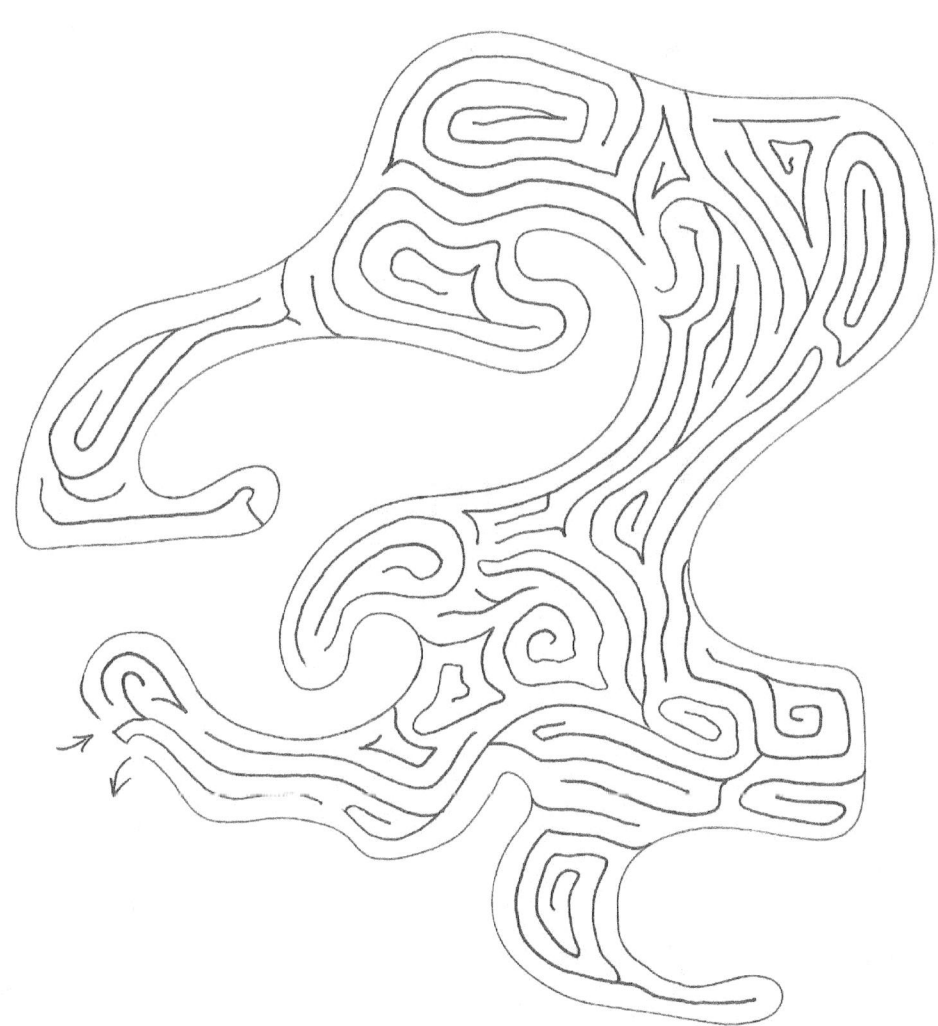

Ink
Swerly
DW

Looking up

30-35 min

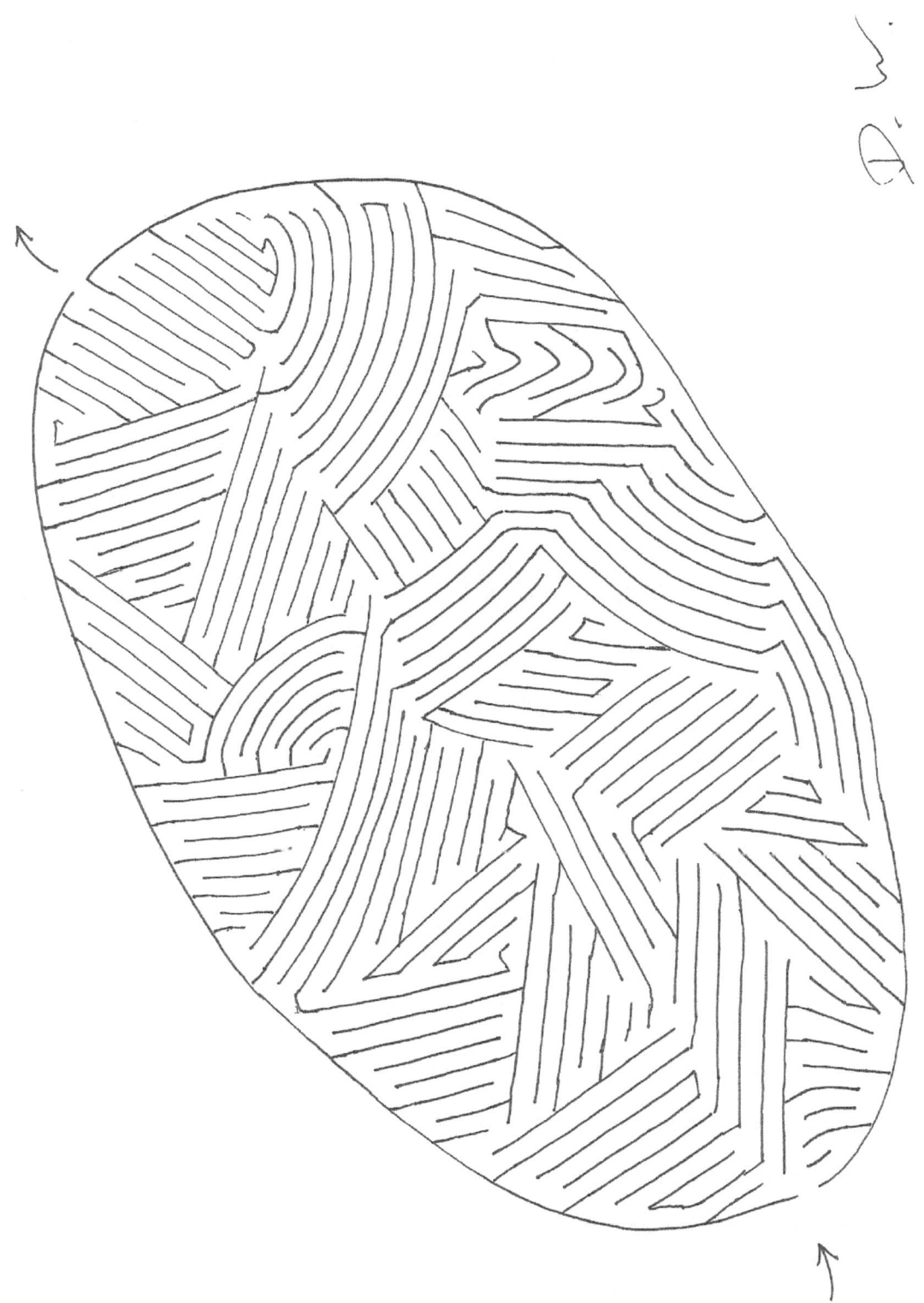

Die Zauberflute

35-40 min

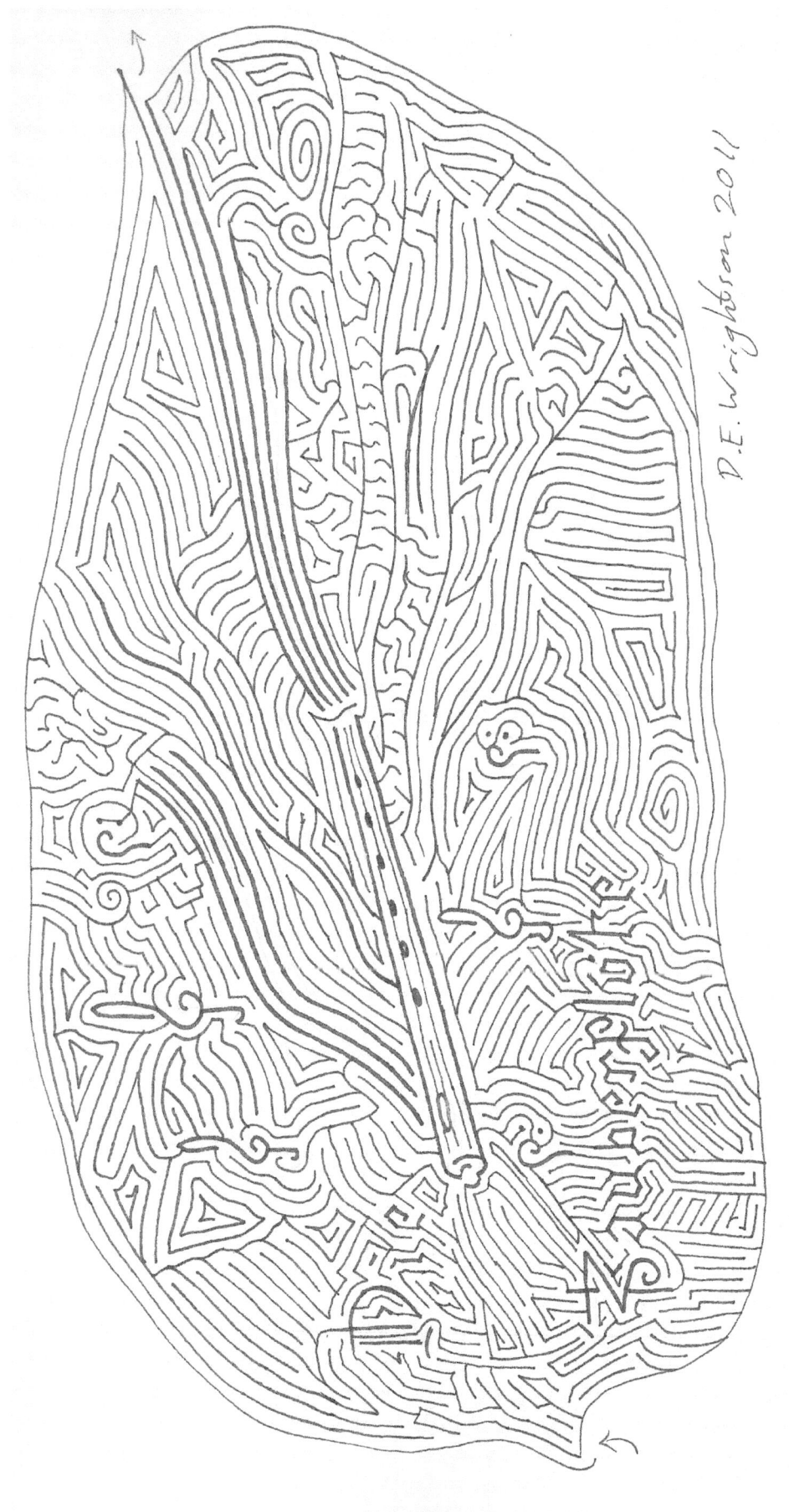

D.E. Wrightson 2011

Wobbly

10-15 min

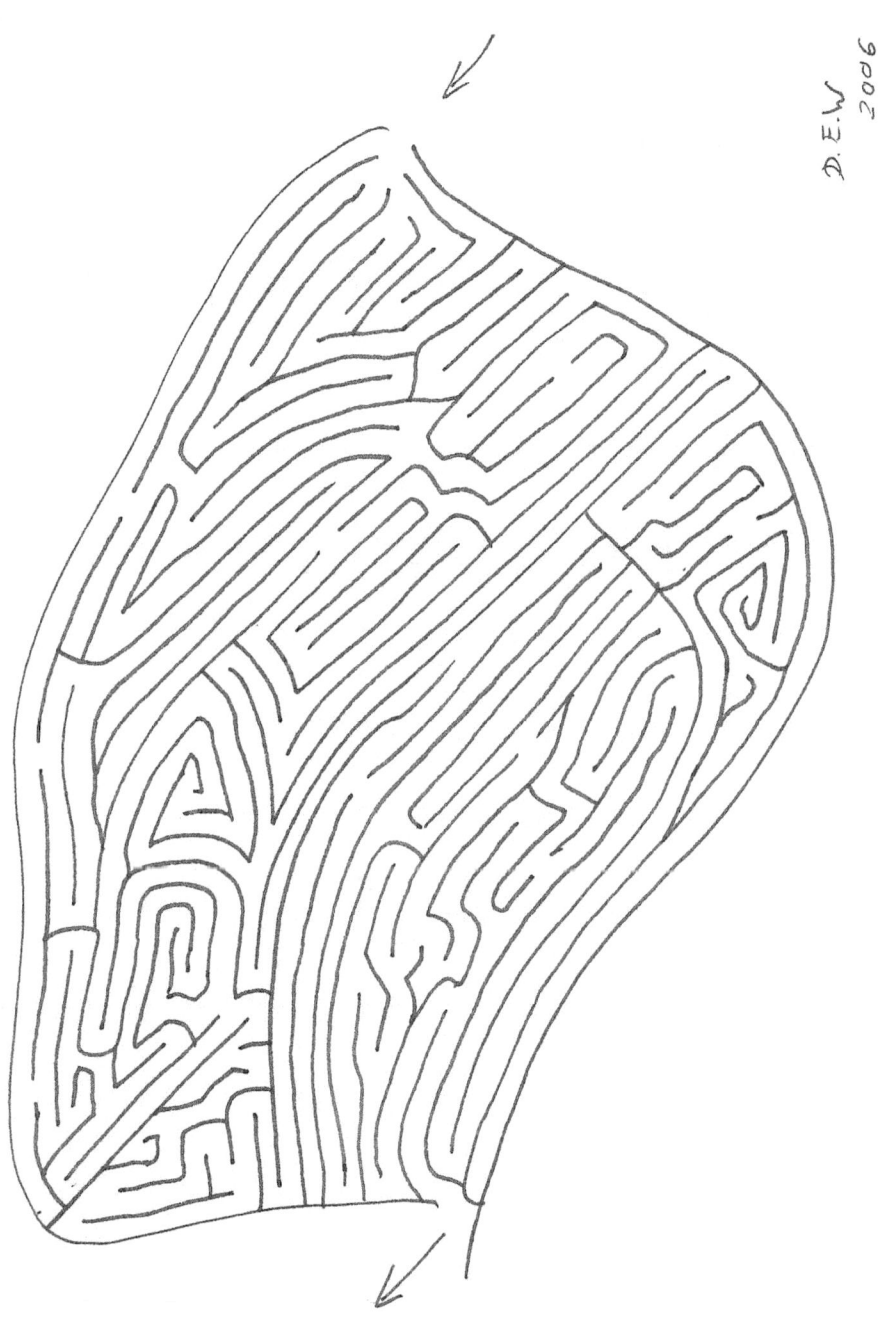

D.E.W
2006

Unicorn Maze

20-30 min

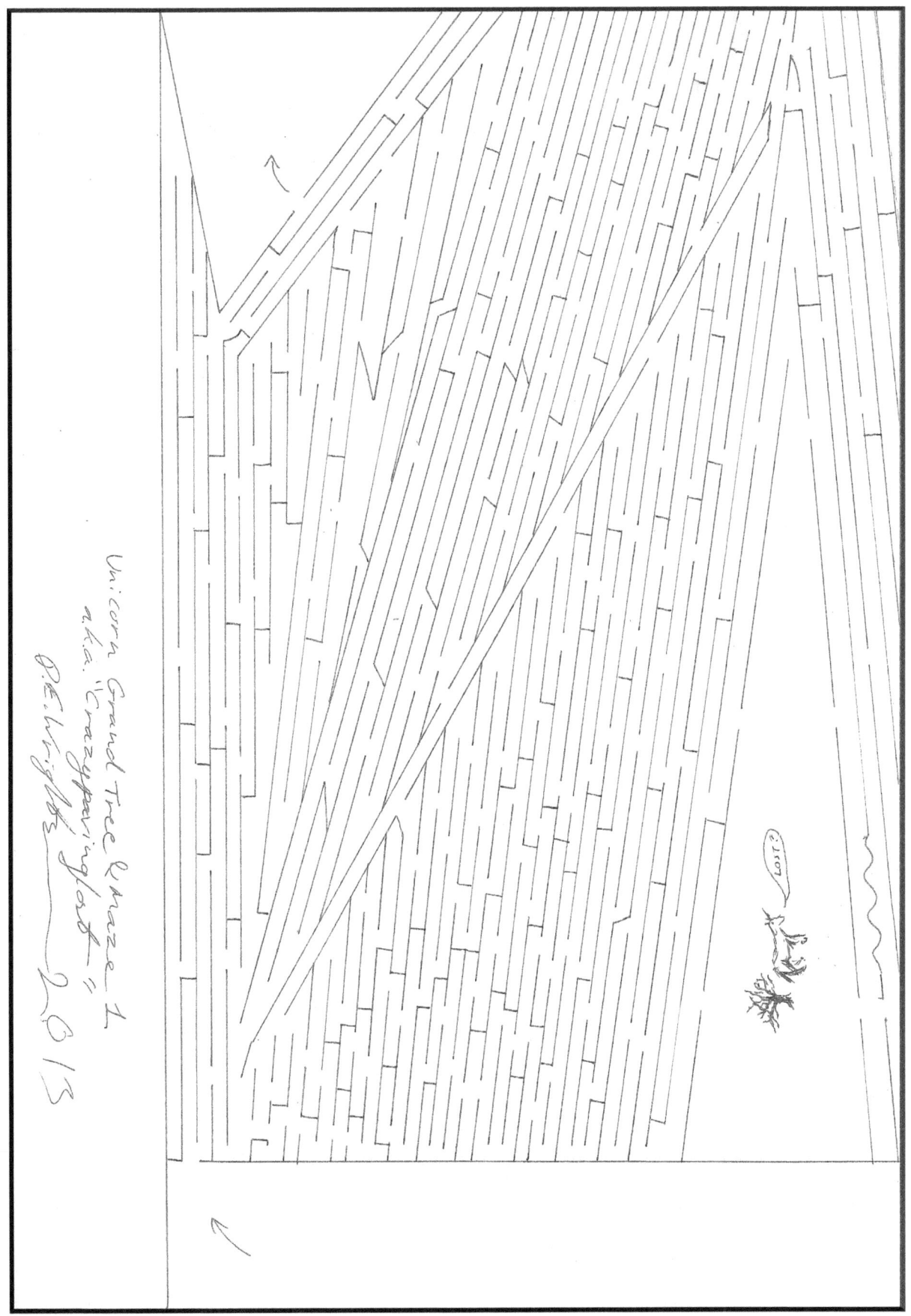

Unicorn Grand Tree Chase 1
a.k.a. "Crazy spring lost"
D.E. Wright 2015

LOST!

Maze

40-50 min

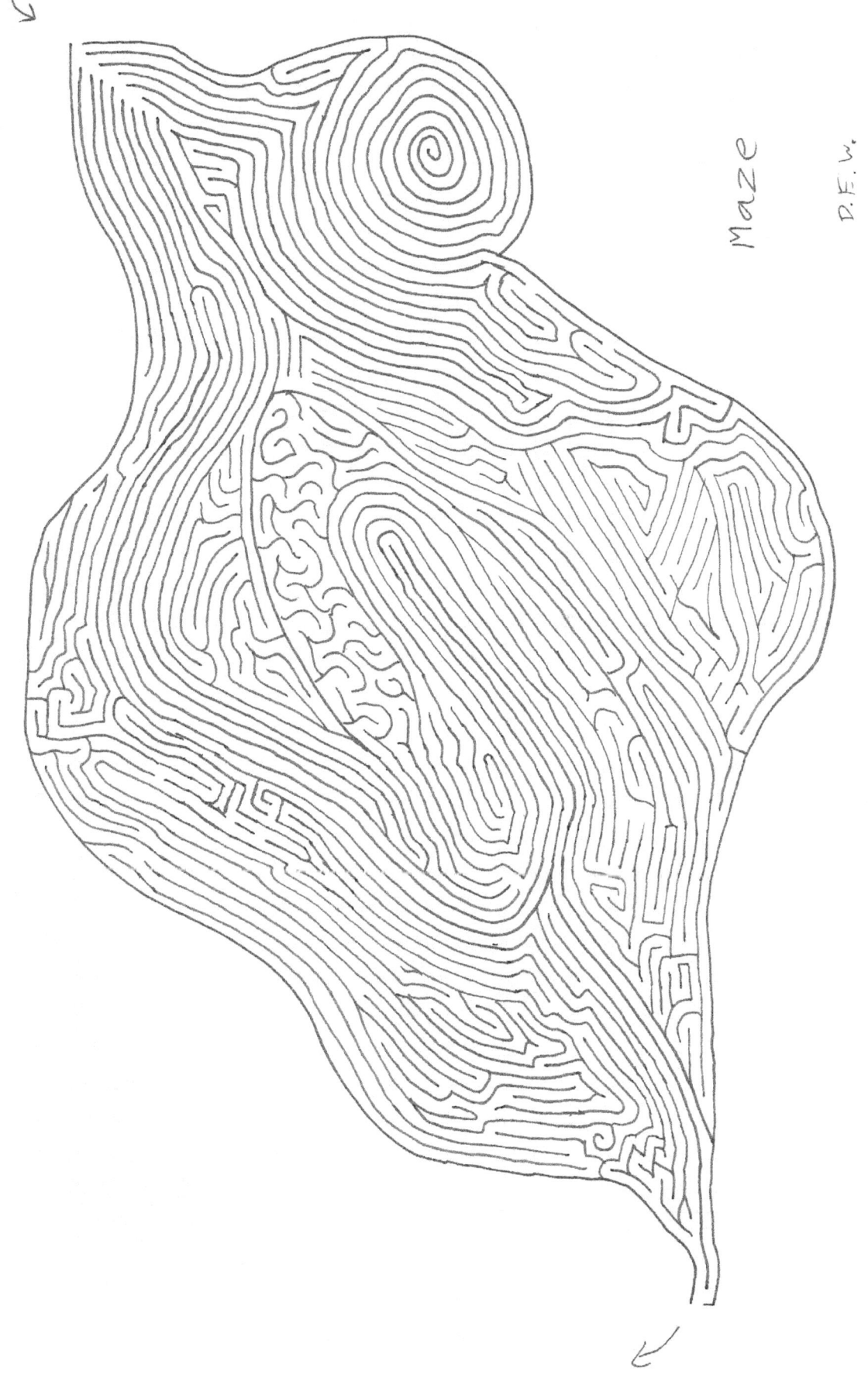

Maze

D.E.W.

Quadragley

10-15 min

Quadragley

D. W.

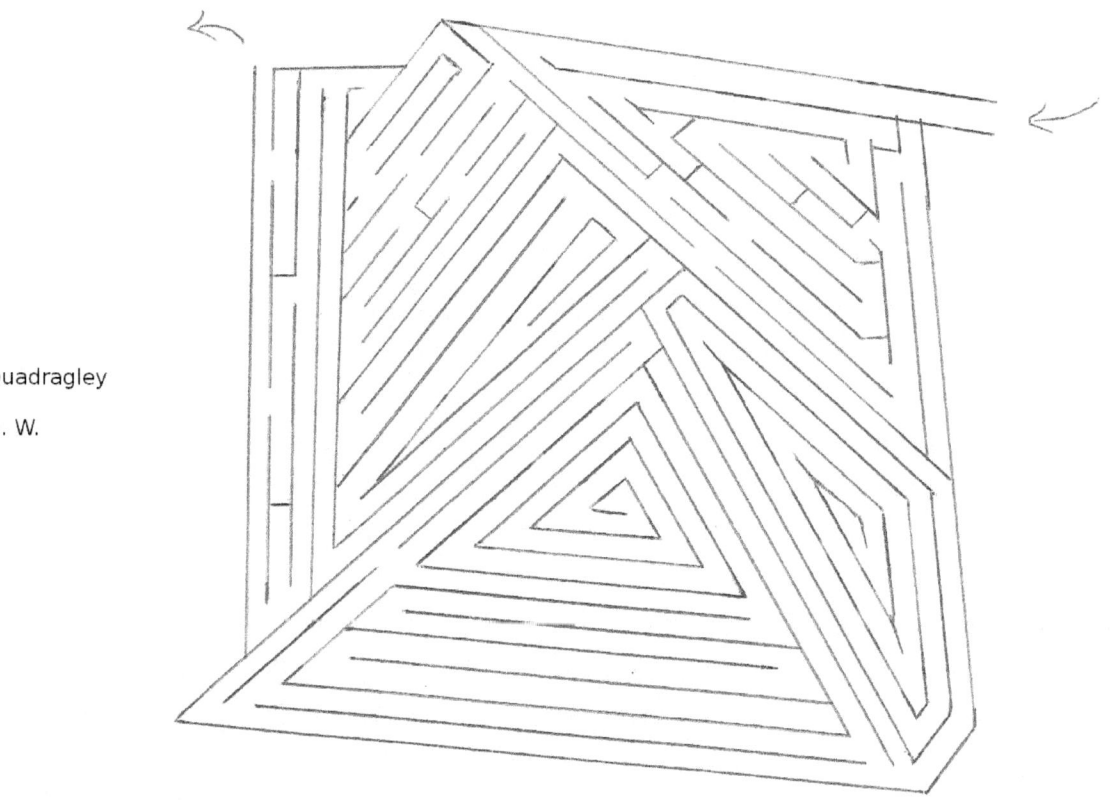

Puff

10-15 min

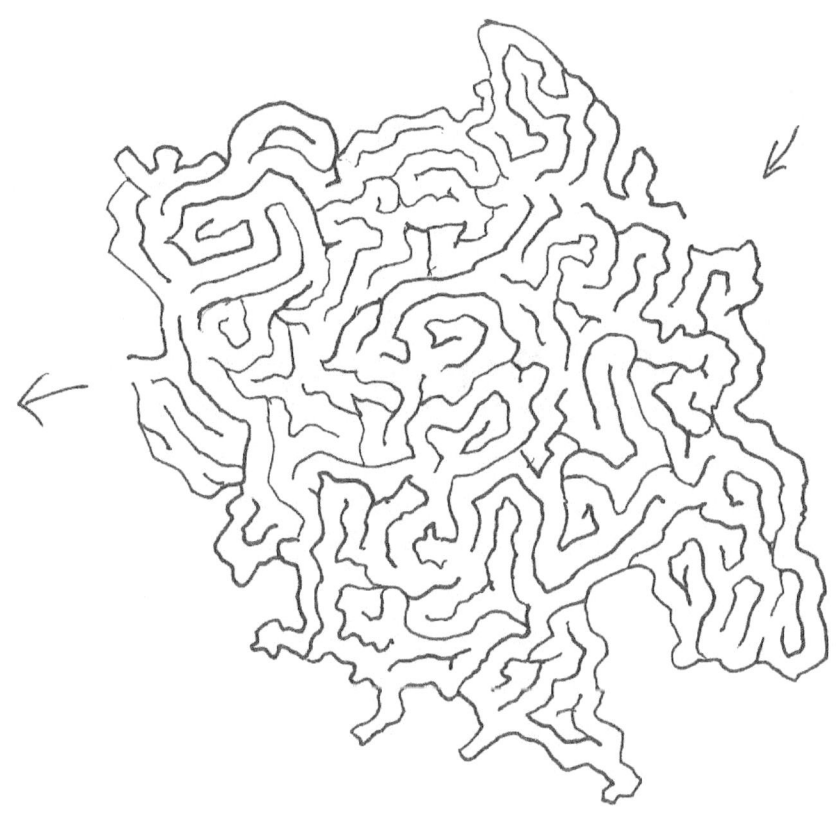

Puff   **D.W.**

Rat Goes Squeek

15-20 min

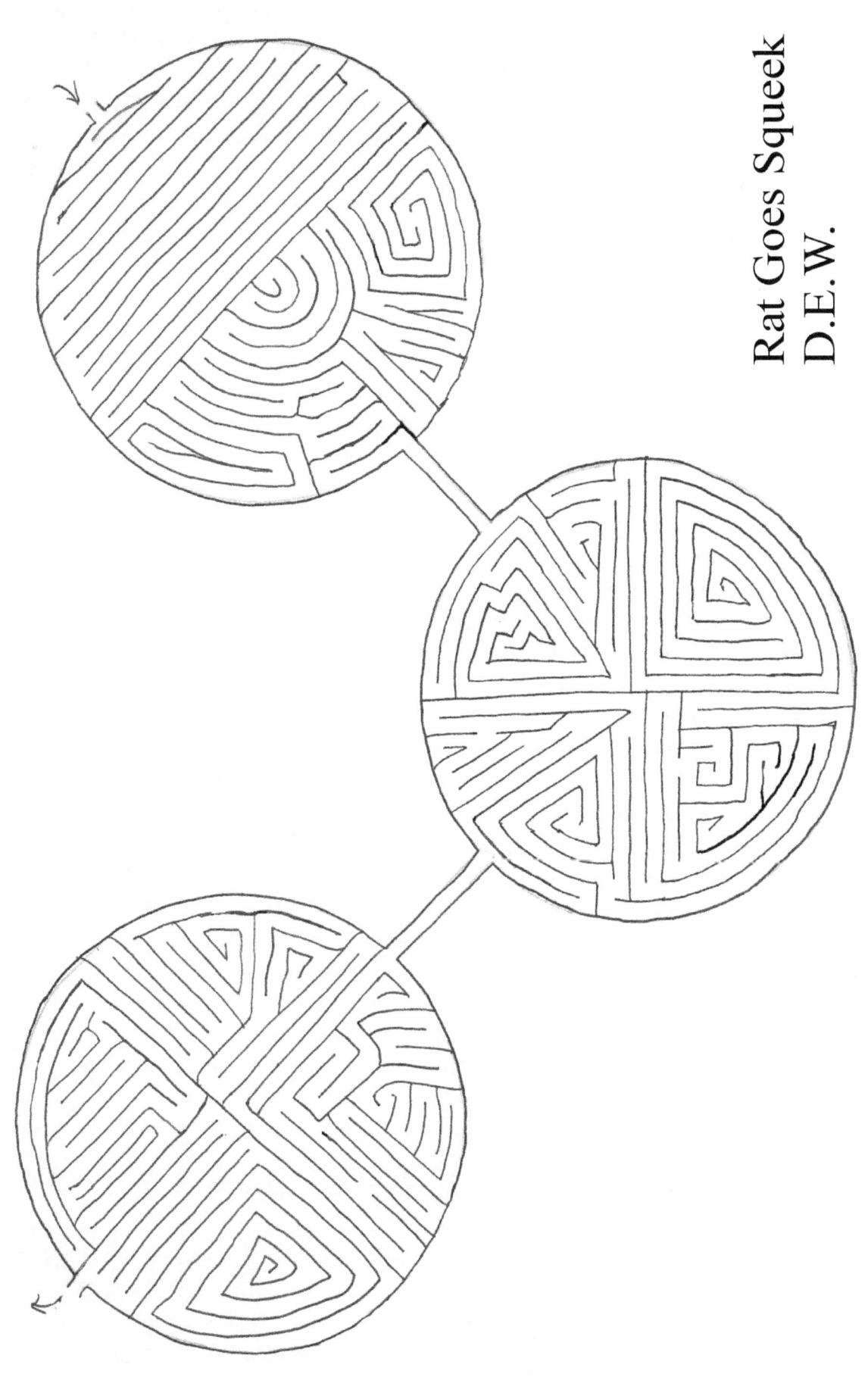

Rat Goes Squeek
D.E.W.

Ripples

35-40 min

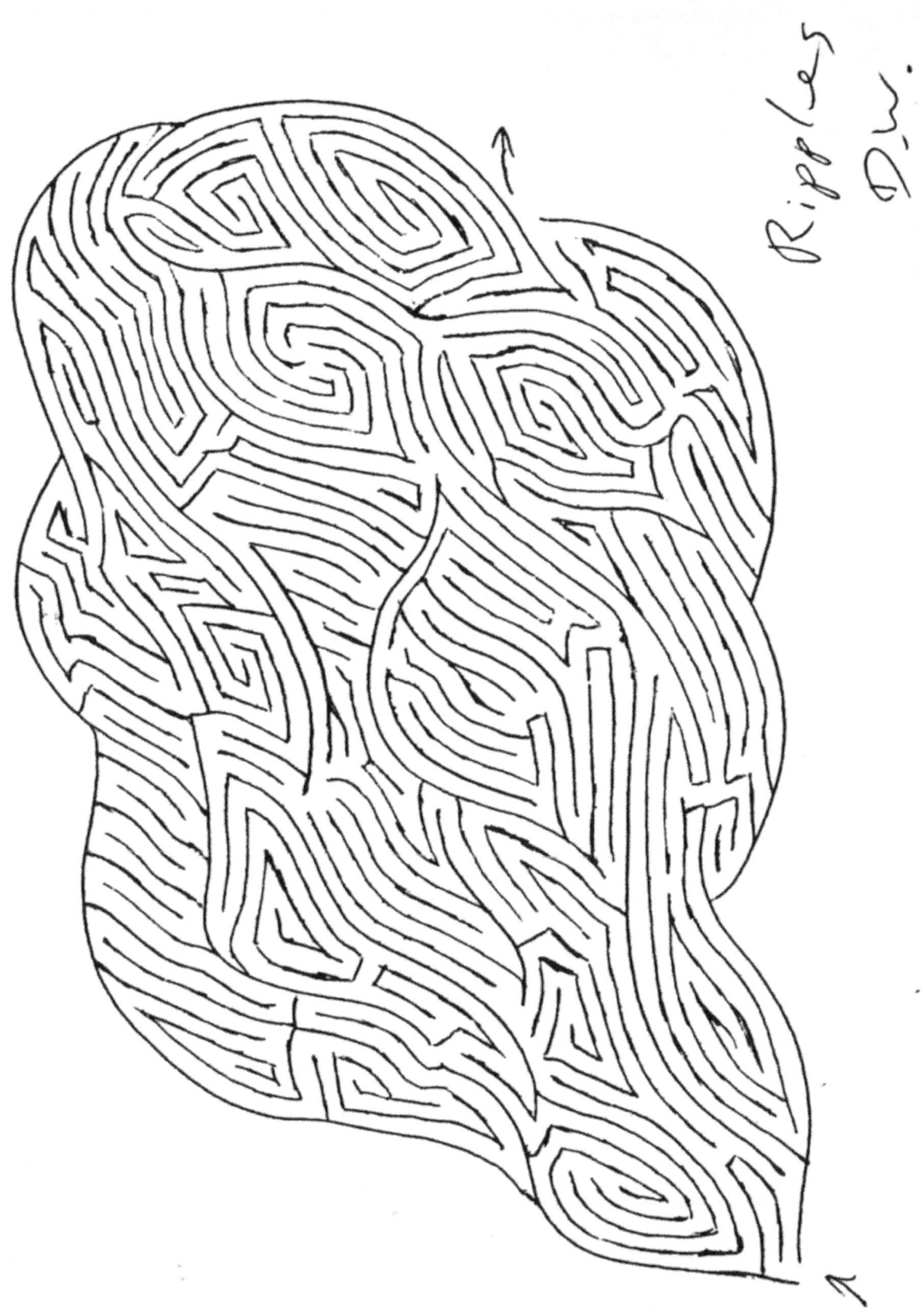

Ripples
D.W.

Firebird

1-2 hours

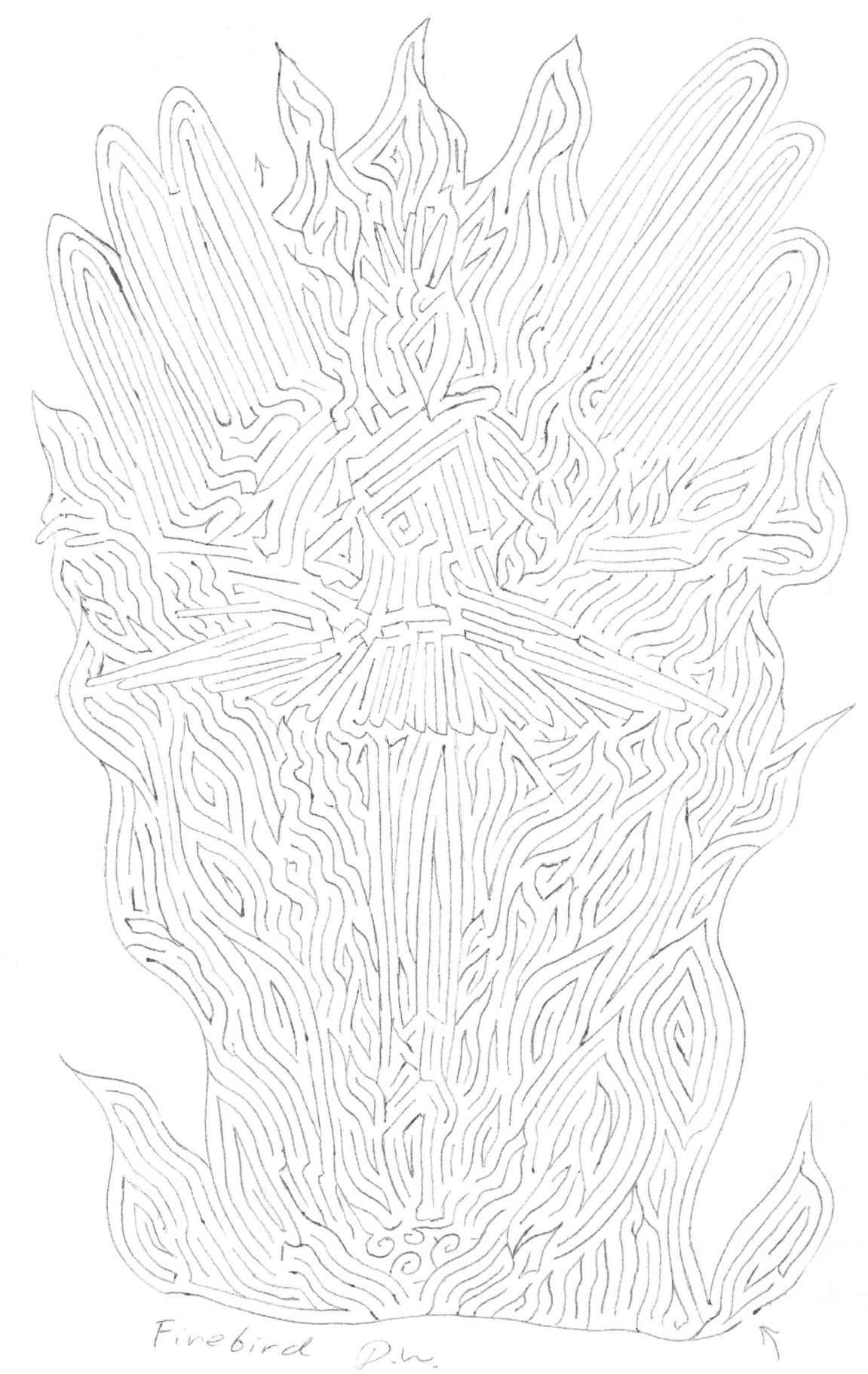

Firebird D.W.

Enjoy!

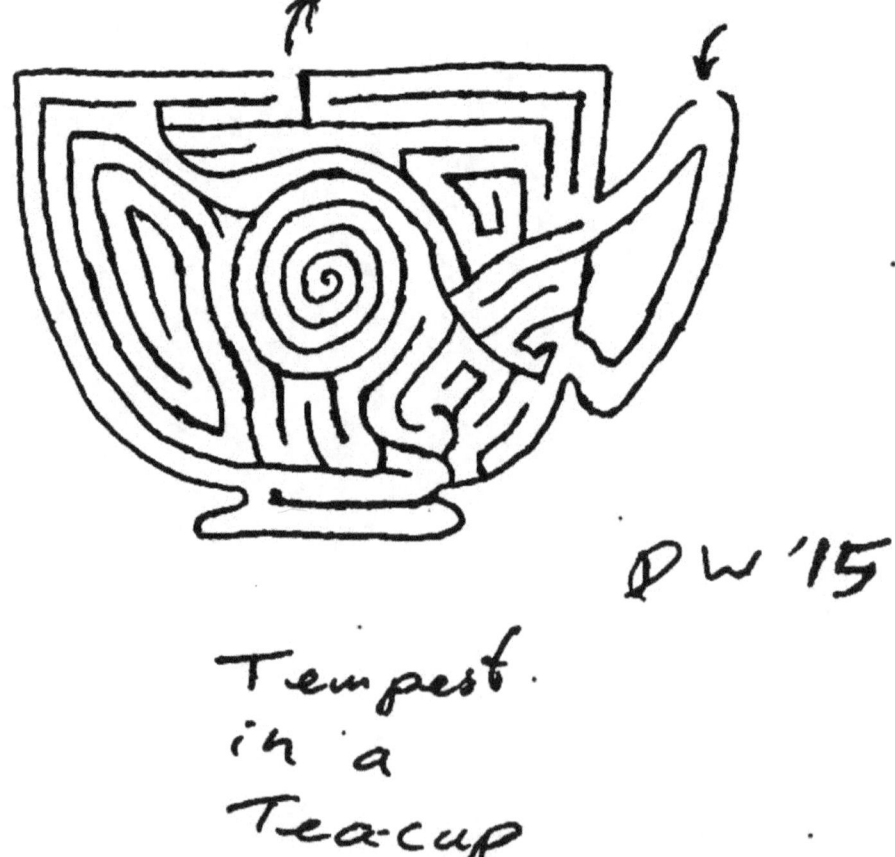

DW '15

Tempest
in a
Teacup